SOCIAL MEDIA MARKETING

Complete Guide to
Social Media Marketing 365
How to Successfully Boost your business
A-Z

Jason Cooper

Table of Contents

Introduction

Congratulations on downloading this book and thank you for doing so.

This book is a comprehensive guide to social media marketing, one of the most important tools for marketers today.

There are plenty of books on this subject on the market; thanks again for choosing this one. Every effort was made to ensure it is full of as much useful information as possible. Please enjoy!

Chapter 1:
What is Social Media Marketing and Why is it Important?

Social media marketing is the combination of two powerful tools: social media, an increasingly common way that information is spread, and marketing, the promotion of products and services. In today's world, where large numbers of people use at least one type of social media, traditional marketing alone no longer reaches consumers as well as it used to. As more and more people get their news online, marketing venues such as television, radio, and print media lose much of their punch. This transition from the marketing techniques of yesterday to newer methods is only going to continue as younger generations, already the most active users of social media, grow older.

Coming up with a great social media marketing strategy for your company is now more important than ever. But what is a great social media marketing strategy, and how do you create the one that best fits your company and its overall marketing strategy?

Deep down, social media marketing is like traditional marketing. It exists to get consumers to spend their time or money on a certain good or service from a specific company. But in many crucial ways, social media marketing isn't like traditional marketing. In the past, companies that bought an advertisement in print media, on television, or on the radio could be reasonably certain that people would see or hear it. Even if consumers used the commercial break to grab a drink or skimmed over an ad in a magazine, chances were that a character, jingle, or image from the advertisement would stick in their minds after they came across it a few times. In other words, marketers had a captive audience.

On social media, consumers are less captive. Social media is like a giant buffet, where people can pick and choose their favorite foods from an endless array of options. They're no longer limited to the channels on their television, the articles in their local newspaper, or the radio stations in their area. They can pick the exact news sources they want, when they want them, and change or add to them at will. Marketers don't have that captive audience any more. Instead, they have to make consumers want to watch, listen to, or read their content. That is the challenge of social media marketing: making promotional content that people actually want to consume.

This might seem like a daunting task, especially if your company is used to the traditional style of marketing. But although social media marketing might be tricky at first, it's not impossible. And the more you practice promoting your goods and services through new social media channels, they better you will become at this new style of marketing. This book is the ultimate guide to creating a great social media marketing campaign that will benefit you and your company.

Chapter 2:
An Overview of Key Social Media Platforms

Just about everyone knows about Facebook, even if they don't have a profile. But Facebook isn't the only social media site out there, and it's certainly not the only social media site you will want to target with your social media marketing campaign. On the other hand, trying to establish a presence on every social media site--or even just the top ten--is exhausting and may not be the best use of your marketing resources.

The next chapter will cover identifying your target demographic and the social media sites that are best suited to that demographic. This chapter will give a brief overview of several of the key social media sites. These sites are fairly reliably among the top sites in the United States and, in many cases, globally. Social media site popularity can always change, so it's a good idea to pay attention to what's new, but this list of sites is an excellent start.

Facebook

The most well-known social media site, Facebook is also one of the most widely used. The site was founded exclusively for college students, but has grown since then to include people of all ages (as long as they're 13 or older). It's not uncommon for kids on Facebook to be "friends" with their parents and even grandparents, as well as people their own age. Facebook's main features include the ability to create a profile containing personal information and the ability to post and share content, including written messages, pictures, and video.

Recently, Facebook added live stream video, allowing its users to share messages in real time. Facebook's key strengths are its wide range and its flexibility as a platform. Few other social media sites attract such a wide variety of users of all ages and backgrounds. And unlike some other social media sites, Facebook supports many different kinds of content.

Written posts can be any length, and there is no size restriction on images or videos. Individuals can create personal profiles, but businesses can also create "pages," which can be "liked" or shared. Facebook users can become members of groups, which can be public or private, connecting them with others with similar interests or experiences. While Facebook is perhaps not the coolest social media site for younger people the way it was a few years ago, the sheer diversity of possibilities and user experiences that Facebook makes possible makes it a valuable social media marketing tool.

Twitter

Twitter users share content in the form of "tweets," short soundbytes of information that are broadcasted to a person's "followers." Twitter's most famous feature is the 140-

character limit imposed on tweets. Since 2016, this limit hasn't included Twitter "handles" (people's usernames, marked with an @ symbol) or content such as videos, gifs, and photos, but users are still limited to short messages on the site. Twitter's next most famous feature is the hashtag, marked by the # symbol. Hashtags summarize the content or theme of a tweet and can be used to link it with other, similar tweets. A hashtag used by a large number of the site's users is said to be "trending." Users create their own hashtags and sometimes personalize them for specific events.

For example, a couple getting married could create the hashtag "#hannah&mark2017" for their wedding, which their guests could use to "tag" any pictures of the celebration that they shared on Twitter. Twitter users share content by "retweeting" other people's tweets, sometimes adding their own commentary. This allows the site to be useful for social activism and the quick spread of information. From a social media marketing perspective, Twitter allows a company to share small, interesting bits of information and create its own personal brand online using tools like hashtags and retweeting other user content.

YouTube

Many people might not think of YouTube as a social media site, but just like Facebook and Twitter, it allows people to share and comment on content. Like Facebook, YouTube has a broad user base. Even people who do not have a YouTube login and who may never even consider posting a video to the site have likely seen a video on YouTube at some point.

The site supports content from professionally created videos to amateur films, audio recordings to visual art, and school projects to beauty tutorials. Some YouTube users post videos regularly, creating a video blog, or vlog. Occasionally, these users will become very

popular, and their videos can receive hundreds of thousands of views. Sometimes this popularity serves as a jumping-off point to stardom in more traditional areas of the media. For your company, YouTube creates the possibility to give consumers a more in-depth look at what you do through videos. Content created for YouTube can also be shared to Facebook and Twitter.

LinkedIn

LinkedIn is a social media site for professionals. Like on Facebook, users create a profile, but rather than listing their interests, family members, and favorite quotes, it acts as a virtual resume. A profile on LinkedIn can include a user's educational and professional experience as well as their skills, volunteer experience, and publications.

LinkedIn allows people to connect with others in their field, network with fellow professionals, and share their work accomplishments. It's also a great site for recruiters, who use it to find people who fit the position they are looking to fill. For companies, LinkedIn is a good resource to connect with other individuals and enterprises in their industry.

Instagram

Instagram is a social media site that primarily focuses on visual content. The site originally supported only pictures, but has since started to allow users to upload video content as well. While it's possible to view a person's Instagram account via a web browser, the site is mostly used via an app. Instagram users can modify their photos or videos with "filters" before posting them. Filters change the lighting, contrast, or coloration of a photo or video, making smartphone photos and videos look better.

Photos and videos can be accompanied by a text description or message, and unlike Twitter, there is no character limit. Like on Twitter, however, Instagram users frequently add hashtags to their posts. Instagram is a great site for social media marketers looking to promote visual content.

Snapchat

Snapchat is a newer social media platform and is only accessible through an app, not through a web browser. Constantly changing and adding new features, it can be a challenging platform to keep up with. However, it can also be a very valuable tool for social media marketers because it reaches some of the youngest users of social media. Snapchat allows users to send pictures, short video clips, or written messages to their contact on the app. These pictures, videos, or messages can only be viewed for a short period of time and then cannot be seen again.

Users can also share pictures or videos to their "story," where they will be visible for 24 hours. One key feature of Snapchat is users' ability to modify their photos and videos. People can add text, drawings, images, filters, and lenses to their photos and videos before sharing them. Some Snapchat filters are similar to Instagram filters and change the composition of the photo or video, while others are "geo-located," or based on the location of the user.

For example, a user visiting the Washington Monument in Washington, D.C. may be able to add a special Washington Monument filter to their Snapchat, while a user visiting the Golden Gate Bridge in San Francisco, California, could add a filter featuring that iconic landmark. Lenses are a Snapchat feature that identifies a user's face and overlays it with an image, such as a hat, sunglasses, or a dog face. These images move with the user and can be added to photos or videos. Other lenses modify the user's features, making their eyes huge, their mouth wide, or any other variety of silly effects. Last but not least for social media marketers, Snapchat has a "Discover" page where news and other organizations can share videos with users. Snapchat isn't an easy social media app to keep up with, but it can be valuable depending on your target demographic.

Pinterest

At first glance, Pinterest looks a bit like the photo sharing site Instagram. However, it's not so much a photo sharing site as a catalog of ideas. Pinterest users "pin" images on themed "boards" much like a scrapbooker might do on a real-world corkboard. The themes of these boards can be anything, including recipes, exercise, fashion, home decor, weddings, travel, parties, holidays, and much more.

The pins that users place on these boards are any images that they want to save and share with others. Some people use Pinterest for practical reasons, such as wedding planning or home redesign.

It's a very convenient place to save pictures of great ideas that a Pinterest user could put to use themselves. Other people use Pinterest to catalog their interest in a topic and connect with others with the same interests. Pinterest can be a great way for a social media marketer to get a company's content online because it is so focused on sharing images. And posts to Pinterest can also be shared on other social media sites.

Chapter 3:
Identifying Your Target Social Media
Marketing Demographic

One of the key components of any marketing campaign is identifying your target demographic. Marketing targeted at teens and young adults isn't going to be the same as marketing targeted at people over 65, which in turn will be different from marketing targeted at people in their thirties. Social media marketing is no different. Just like in a traditional marketing campaign, the content of a social media marketing campaign has to change depending on its target demographic. Additionally, however, for social media marketing, the target demographic determines the social media platform that is most useful for the campaign.

In many ways, this isn't so different from traditional marketing. Marketers probably wouldn't place a television ad for clothing aimed at college students in the commercial break after a daytime game show, but they might successfully market a home exercise machine in the same spot.

It's all about finding where your audience is: college students probably aren't watching daytime game shows because they have to be in class. Retired people, on the other hand, are much more likely to be watching television at this time of day, and they are more likely to be interested in a home exercise machine than a clothing line aimed at people decades younger.

Social media is no different. As the previous chapter showed, social media sites are very diverse and attract very different audiences. While some social media platforms reach a wide variety of people (Facebook), others are much more specific (Snapchat). Here are some tips for identifying the best social media platform for your social media marketing campaign, based on your target demographic.

If your target demographic is 65+

You might have some trouble reaching this older demographic on social media because they are the group that uses social media the least, but it can't hurt to try. Many people have a tech savvy parent or grandparent, and the percentage of older people active on social media will only grow as time passes. Right now, Facebook is your best bet when trying to target this demographic.

Older people who might be less interested in the news- and information-sharing capabilities of Twitter, less attracted to the visual content of Instagram and Pinterest, retired and therefore not on LinkedIn, and unswayed by the immediacy of Snapchat still often see the utility of Facebook as a way of keeping in touch with far away family and old friends.

YouTube is another social media platform that, used in conjunction with Facebook, can be useful for targeting the 65+ demographic. YouTube videos are straightforward to watch and can be shared on Facebook, giving your company some flexibility in marketing.

If your target demographic is older but not retired

Like for the 65+ group, Facebook is a great social media platform for marketing to an older, but not yet retired, demographic. Many people in this group have grown children who are at college or out on their own and they use Facebook to keep in touch. Many have also discovered the fun of reconnecting with old classmates, distant relatives, and childhood friends that they had lost touch with over the years.

Having had more experience with technology, they are also more likely to consume and share more informative or viral content online. Some members of this demographic may be on Twitter, and many may also be found on LinkedIn, since they are still professionally active. A presence on all three of these sites is a good social media marketing technique for targeting this demographic.

If your target demographic is people in their thirties and forties

While many people in their thirties and forties did not grow up using online technology and social media, they were some of its earliest adopters. In fact, the original members of Facebook are now part of this group. Many people in this demographic are comfortable on social media. They have profiles on Facebook and LinkedIn.

They use Twitter both personally and professionally. They watch (and maybe post) videos on YouTube. A few might even use Pinterest, Instagram, and Snapchat. In terms of social media marketing, while a presence on LinkedIn and YouTube is always useful, Facebook and Twitter are key for this demographic. Many people in this group are starting families and are using Facebook to keep in touch with old friends and share news updates with far away extended family members.

They are also concerned with the news, global events, and politics because they and their children are more likely to be directly affected for decades to come. Twitter is a good platform for these topics, and is also commonly used for professional networking and information sharing. By focusing on Facebook and Twitter, a social media marketer can best target this demographic.

If your target demographic is people in their twenties

People in their twenties often started using social media in their early teens. Many had MySpace, followed by Facebook. They adopted Twitter, Instagram, Pinterest, and Snapchat as those platforms became popular, and created profiles on LinkedIn as they joined the workforce. Over all, people in their twenties are some of the most active and broad users of social media. They use social media for personal as well as professional reasons.

They are often on social media daily, and they get much of their news from online sources, frequently filtered through social media. Many do their shopping online. This group is an important target demographic for companies because they are more likely to be reached through social media than through traditional marketing methods. If a person gets their news and entertainment online, they will watch less television, listen to less radio, and read fewer newspapers and magazines.

To market to people like this, companies need to reach them where they are, and they are on social media. This is especially important because, as this demographic grows older and becomes the thirty- to forty-year-old demographic and then the retirement age demographic, they are unlikely to stop using social media and start using more traditional forms of news and entertainment. In order to continue to appeal to this group, companies have to learn how to use social media marketing.

Since the young professional and twenty-something demographic uses social media broadly, companies have more choice in what platforms they would like to use. Facebook is a great option because many people in this group have been using Facebook for many years and are very comfortable with the platform. However, companies can get an edge by using more niche platforms such as Instagram, Pinterest, and even Snapchat. In the case of Instagram and Pinterest, content posted on those platforms can be shared on Facebook as well as Twitter. This interoperability of social media platforms, which will be discussed in more detail later in the book, is important to creating a well-rounded and influential social media marketing campaign.

If your target demographic is teens

After over a decade of near social media dominance, Facebook is losing steam with the youngest social media users. Today's teens often have a Facebook profile, but it's not to

keep up with their friends. Instead, they have Facebook because it is a broad platform that helps them keep in touch with a larger group of people, such as extended family.

Ironically, Grandma gets Facebook to keep up with the grandkids, while the grandkids get Facebook because Grandma's on it. Teens today keep in touch with their friends using other social media platforms. Twitter, Instagram, and Snapchat are very popular. In comparison to Facebook, it can be harder to create social media marketing content for these platforms, particularly Snapchat. Twitter is very responsive to trends, and keeping up with those trends can be challenging. Instagram relies on visual content, which is more difficult to create than text content alone. And Snapchat can be confusing to learn and challenging to keep up with.

However, a social media marketing campaign targeting one or all of these platforms can be very beneficial in terms of attracting the attention of today's youngest consumers. Like people in their twenties, this group is unlikely to start consuming news and information from traditional media sources as they grow older. Many are "digital natives," having used online technology since they were young children. Teens are inherently a difficult group to market to because they are so attuned to ever-changing trends. A company that can attract them where they are, social media, can really benefit.

Chapter 4:
Sharing Content on Social Media 101

Maybe you've used Facebook, tweeted, or uploaded a video to YouTube. But perhaps you've never seen an Instagram, pinned an image on Pinterest, or watched somebody's snap story. If you're not sure how to get started on these social media platforms, this chapter is for you. Step by step, it will get you up to speed creating, posting, and sharing content.

Facebook

If you don't already have one, create a page on Facebook for your company. In the past, if you wanted to have a company presence on Facebook you had to create a profile for your company, just like your own personal profile.

Then, Facebook created pages. Pages are similar to profiles except that, instead of other users becoming "friends" with your company, they can now "like" it and follow its posts. This allows Facebook and its users to better differentiate between people with profiles and companies (or music groups, public figures, televisions shows, etc.) with pages. If your company has its own profile, switch it over to a page. It's a bit more professional and more in line with what other companies are doing.

To create a page, follow these steps:

1. Go to www.facebook.com. At the bottom of the page, click on "Create a page."

2. Choose a page type. If you're not sure, choose the page type that fits best with the sort of brand you aspire to be. Enter the required information. It's good to provide accurate and complete information because consumers will use your Facebook page for information. (You will need to be logged in to your own Facebook account to complete this step. All pages are managed from an individual's Facebook account. If you don't have a Facebook account, create one before getting started with creating a page.)

3. Add information to your page. Choose page and cover photos that look nice and showcase what your company does. Don't forget to add a short description so that people coming across your page for the first time will be able to find out who you are and what you do.

4. Create content! Facebook gives you several options for posts from your new page. This is where you can get creative and let your company's strengths shine. You can post traditional text posts, with or without tags, hashtags, or colored backgrounds. You can also post photo albums or videos. Facebook also supports the ability to live stream video.

5. There are multiple ways to post content to Facebook, but all of the options are available from your home page. Tap or click the text bar that says "What's on your mind?" From here, you can add a photo or video, identify a place, tag friends, or several other options. If you tap or click the photo and video option, it will allow you to choose a photo or video from your files or take a new one.

6. If you want to post a live video on Facebook, follow the same steps, but choose "Live Video" from the list of options. You can add a description to your video. Next, tap or click "Go Live" and start your video. When you are done, tap or click "Finished." Live videos are available to your followers as they are being filmed, but they can also be re-watched afterwards.

7. Depending on your page's privacy settings, your posts may only be visible to people who are following you. It's not a bad idea to make your posts visible to everyone, not only people who have liked your page. You can change your privacy settings to make all future posts public. You can also click on the arrow to the right of a specific post, choose the option to modify the post, choose the privacy settings, and change the visibility to public. This way, your posts will reach more people who have not encountered your brand before.

Twitter

Unlike on Facebook, company and individual Twitter profiles are the same. If you're already using Twitter, you can use the same process to sign up for a company account as you used to sign up for your personal account. Just use a different email address, preferably a generic company email.

1. Go to www.twitter.com and click on "Sign Up."

2. Enter a name, email, and password in the fields provided. This can be your company name.

3. Add a phone number to your account, if you want.

4. Create a username. This will become your Twitter "handle," or the phrase that comes after the @ sign when you tweet or people tweet at you. It can be hard to find a username that isn't taken since so many people use Twitter, so don't become too attached to a single possibility. That said, try to make your handle relevant to your brand. You don't want a random combination of letters and numbers that no one will remember. Get creative!

5. Choose some Twitter feeds to follow. Twitter thrives on connections, and your presence on Twitter will grow faster if you are interacting with other Twitter users. To get started, pick some well-known companies and people in your field to follow. You can always follow more feeds later.

6. Import your contacts, if you want. This might not work as well for a company Twitter feed as it would for a personal one, since your contacts might not be using the same email address for their Twitter as they do for their professional email.

7. When you get to your new home page, click on your username and go to your Twitter profile. Add a profile picture and a cover photo. You can also write a short bio, include your location, and connect to a website. These are all good things to do for your company to get started on Twitter.

8. Start tweeting! Remember to include hashtags and keep your posts under 140 characters.

YouTube

Getting started on YouTube is easy now because YouTube accounts are automatically connected with Gmail accounts. Anyone with a Gmail can use it to log in to YouTube and post videos. Again, it's important here to use a generic company email. If your company doesn't use Gmail, you can create one for free to use with YouTube and simply set it up to forward all messages to a company email.

1. Go to www.youtube.com. If you are already logged in to Gmail, your profile icon will show in the top right corner. If you aren't, click "Sign In." If you're logged in to a Gmail account that you don't want to use with YouTube, sign out and log in to the correct Gmail account.

2. Once you are logged in to the correct account, click the "Upload" button in the top right corner. It's a little upward-facing arrow. This will bring you to a page where you create your YouTube channel. You can change the name that pops up

automatically if you would like, and you can specifically create your channel for a business. Then click "Create Channel."

3. Upload videos! YouTube will also help you create slideshows and edit your videos. There's also the possibility to live stream video.

LinkedIn

Like on Facebook, you have to have a personal profile on LinkedIn in order to create a page for your company on the site. If you don't have a personal LinkedIn profile, go to www.linkedin.com to create one before beginning these steps.

1. From your own LinkedIn home page, click the "Work" icon in the top right corner. A menu will appear. Choose "Show More" from the bottom of this menu. From there, choose "Create a Company Page."

2. Enter your company's name into the fields that appear. You will need to have a verifiable work email address and check the box that confirms that you have the right to create this page for your company. Click "Continue."

3. Enter the rest of your company's information. You may need to confirm the email address you used. You will also need to add a company description and the URL of your company's website. If you don't have a company website, now is a great time to create one as well.

4. When you are ready, publish your page! Make sure you also have profile and cover photos. If you are using Facebook, Twitter, or any other site that has

profile and cover photos, it's not a bad idea to use the same ones. This creates a unified image for your company.

Instagram

Instagram, like Snapchat, is primarily a smartphone application. It's possible to view Instagram content on a web browser, but the app is designed to work best with a smartphone.

1. Download the Instagram app on the smartphone you want to use. Open the app and follow the prompts to set up your account. Use your business name as the first and last name, and create a username that reflects your company. Make sure to add a profile photo. It's never a bad idea to use the same photo that you use on other social media platforms, but since Instagram is very visually oriented, you can also use a more artistic or classically beautiful photo.

2. Find people to follow. Instagram will probably suggest some people you know. You can also search for other users. Remember that if you follow others, they are more likely to follow you back!

3. Add photos or videos. You can swipe right from the home screen to open the camera, or tap the box with the plus sign at the bottom of the page. The second option also allows you to choose a picture from your phone's camera roll to post. You may have to crop the photo.

4. Add filters and edit your photo. Instagram's most famous feature is its filters, a seemingly endless array of overlay options that change the composition of photos taken on or uploaded to the app. Feel free to choose a filter that makes your

picture look better, brighter, or an overall better representation of your brand. If you want

5. more control, Instagram also allows you to do your own editing. You can customize your photos and videos to make them look their best.

6. After you are done editing, tap "Next." Now, add extra information to your picture. You can write text to accompany a photo, and unlike on Twitter, there's no character limit. You can also add a place tag, such as your business's address and identify other people in the picture. Finally, Instagram makes it easy to cross-post.

You can share your picture to Facebook, Twitter, and several other social media platforms directly from Instagram. When you are ready, tap "Publish." You've posted your first photo on Instagram!

Snapchat

There are several ways to use Snapchat in a social media marketing campaign. It is possible to partner with Snapchat on a more traditional advertising campaign, as the app now includes advertisements, sponsored lenses, and sponsored geofilters. If you are interested in these options, go to www.snapchat.com/ads to learn more about partnering with Snapchat. If you're not looking for a full-blown ad campaign but simply want to get your company out there on Snapchat, try purchasing an on-demand geofilter or simply having a company Snap Story that is public for all viewers.

Purchase an on-demand geofilter:

1. Go to www.snapchat.com/geofilters and choose the "On-Demand" option. If you think you might qualify for a "Community" geofilter, feel free to choose that option, but no brand logos are allowed.

2. Design your geofilter. If you or someone in your company has artistic talent, feel free to design your own geofilter. This also might be a good time to involve a graphic designer, if you can. Otherwise, Snapchat makes it easy by providing a number of templates you can use to design your geofilter.

3. Set a geofence and a time for your geofilter. A geofence determines where Snapchat users can see and use your filter. You don't want to have too small of a geofence because then it will only reach a small number of people. However, you don't want to make your geofence too large, either, or it will not be as relevant to Snapchat users. Choose your time frame carefully. Perhaps your company gets more business on weekends. Use your geofilter then. Or maybe you're having a big event or a sale. That's another good time to use a geofilter. Keeping your geofilter relatively exclusive will keep it from becoming boring to users, too.

4. Pay and submit your geofilter for review. Snapchat does have guidelines for the geofilters it accepts, and it promises that your geofilter will be reviewed within one business day. Your geofilter might not be accepted the first time, but keep trying. It's a fun, worthwhile way to engage with people on Snapchat.

Create a public Snap Story:

1. You'll need a Snapchat account to create a Snap Story, and you'll need a smartphone to create a Snapchat account. First, download the Snapchat app with your smartphone and follow the prompts to create an account. Make sure to choose a username that reflects your company. This is especially important if users want to search for your company on the app.

2. Use the camera on Snapchat to take a photo or video. You can use your regular phone camera or your front-facing phone camera. Then add text, a drawing, or a filter. If you want to add a lens, before taking the picture, hold your finger down on a face in the photo. The available lenses will appear and you can swipe through them and choose one. Then take a photo or video with the lens activated.

3. Add the Snap to your Story by tapping the box with the small cross at the bottom of the photo screen, or by tapping the blue circle with an arrow and then choosing "My Story" on the next page. Then tap the arrow at the bottom of the screen again.

4. By default, your Snap Story is only visible to your friends on Snapchat. If you've just joined Snapchat, you probably don't have any friends, so you will want to set your Story to "public" so more people can see it. To do this, choose the "Settings" gear icon on your home page (swipe down on the photo screen to get to this page).

   Scroll down to the section entitled "Who Can…" and choose "View My Story." Change the selected option from "Friends" to "Everyone." Now your Story is public.

5. Publish more Snap Stories! Snapchat is a great app for sharing candid moments and you can create an entire narrative by taking short videos and photos and

posting them to your Story. Users are attracted to Snapchat because of its candid nature, so make the most of that when you post content on the app.

6. All Snaps published to your Story will disappear 24 hours after they were posted. If you want to delete a Snap from your Story, or if you posted one by accident, go to your Snap Story and tap the three vertical dots at the far right side of the screen. A list of the Snaps that are currently part of your story will appear.

7. Tap the Snap you want to delete. That Snap will show on your screen. At the bottom of the screen, tap the trash can icon and then confirm that you would like to delete that Snap. You can also use this method to see how many people have viewed your Snap. Just tap the eyeball icon at the bottom left of the screen instead of the trash can icon.

Pinterest

Pinterest has different account types for individuals and companies. Your first step in using Pinterest for social media marketing is to set up a business Pinterest rather than a personal account.

1. Go to www.pinterest.com/business/create and fill out the field, then click "Create Account." Including your website is optional, but it's never a bad idea. The big difference between Pinterest for businesses and Pinterest for individuals is that

business accounts get extra features like analytics tools, which are helpful to see how your Pinterest account is doing.

2. Set up your profile. Pinterest will prompt you to choose some accounts to follow in order to create your personalized home page. This is a good opportunity to do some Pinterest networking, choosing accounts that are similar to your own. The more information you include on your profile, the more interesting and relevant you will be to other Pinterest users.

3. Once you are finished setting up your Pinterest account, you will be taken to your home feed, which shows pins from the other accounts that you followed earlier. To create any content on Pinterest, you will need to make a Board. Go to your profile and click "Create Board."

4. Fill out the information in the pop-up to create a Board. Much of the information, including the name, description, and category, is optional, but it's important to fill it all out because that helps other Pinterest users find your Board and your content.

   It's possible to create a shared Board. Just go to the "Collaborators" option at the bottom of the pop-up and add the names of other Pinterest users. They will also be able to add Pins to the Board you have created. Click "Create" and your Board is ready to go!

5. Just like the much more low-tech cork board, Boards on Pinterest are where you put Pins, in this case images. To add a Pin, either go to the Board you would like to pin it to and click "Add a Pin" or go to your home page and click the circle with the plus sign in it at the top of the page. You can upload a Pin from your computer or add one from the Web. Add a description to your Pin and click "Create." If you've added

   a Pin from the Web, your Pin will link back to the website it came from. Again, a great networking technique.

6. It's also possible to share content from other Pinterest users. This is called "re-pinning." When you find a Pin you would like to re-pin, hover over it and click the "Pin It" button that appears. From there, you'll be able to choose which Board you would like to add the Pin to and modify the Pin's description if you would like.

7. Interaction with other Pinterest users doesn't just have to be in the form of re-pinning their content. You can also like and comment on a Pin, send a Pin to someone (even if they're not on Pinterest), tag another Pinterest user, or send another user a message. Using these features to promote other brands helps put your brand out there on Pinterest.

8. Pinterest has a great feature for businesses called "Rich Pins." You'll have to add some metadata to your site and apply to get your Rich Pins validated with Pinterest before you can use them, but it can be well worth it for your company. Rich Pins include extra information, and there are six different types: Place Pins, Article Pins, Product Pins, Recipe Pins, Movie Pins, and App Pins. To learn more about Rich Pins and getting started using them, go to the Pinterest Developer's Page at developers.pinterest.com/docs/rich-pins/overview/?.

These instructions should get you started with social media marketing on some of the top social media sites. If you run into any problems, help is often just an internet search away, and most of these platforms have robust help sites where users can

troubleshoot issues they are having. In the next few chapters, we'll cover what to put on social media. Getting set up on a platform is an excellent first step, but it is just the first step. Great social media marketing requires great content, too, and this book is here to help with that!

Chapter 5:
The Shareability Factor,
or How to Create Great Content

The last few chapters have discussed different types of social media and the demographics that use those social media platforms. But knowing who to target and where isn't the biggest challenge of social media marketing. In this chapter, we'll address that most important factor: content.

In traditional marketing, it was often enough to get people to consume whatever marketing content was produced. If a marketing campaign could get people talking about it, that was even better, but it wasn't essential. On social media, so much content is produced on a daily basis that a marketing campaign that only gets views will get buried.

Successful social media marketing gets *shared*. This is the brilliance of social media marketing: your consumers do your work for you. The challenge of social media marketing, however, is that your consumers will only do your work for you if your content is good enough.

Just about everyone has seen a viral video. These short clips of often unintentionally funny circumstances or events get shared rapidly, crisscrossing the internet until they become a sort of cultural event. Everybody has seen them or heard of them. News media will do a segment on them or write an article about them. Their subjects might get an interview, or several. "Going viral" is the holy grail of marketing.
Views on a single viral video might number in the hundreds of thousands. For a social media marketing team, the idea of reaching that quantity of people with some kind of promotional content is awfully exciting. But the formula for making something go viral remains elusive.

Many viral videos were not meant to go viral at all. They may have been products of sheer luck, where a video camera was running in the right place at the right time. They may have been created intentionally, but without the goal of reaching so many people. They are highly variable. Trying too hard to make a viral video may result in exactly that: a video that makes it seem like you are trying too hard to go viral. And there's another quality of viral videos that marketers should remember: they disappear almost as soon as they appear. For a week or two, they predominate social media and maybe traditional media as well. Everyone knows about them. And then they fade into obscurity. Views, instead of ticking upwards rapidly, stagnate.

Their subjects no longer appear on television or, importantly, on social media. Very few people who become famous because of a viral video stay famous. It is the ultimate incidence of "fifteen minutes of fame." Successful social media marketing needs more than fifteen minutes of fame to succeed. In other words, if your company can create content that goes viral, do it. But don't rely on it. In the long term, you will be better served by social media marketing that creates a solid and expanding base of consumers rather than a huge, short-lived number of views.

So how do you create that solid consumer base? There are three keys to developing social media marketing content that attracts a following: *relevant* material, *quality* material, and material that *tells a story*.

Relevance

The content you produce as part of your social media marketing campaign has to be relevant to your consumers. This is why identifying your target demographic and the accompanying social media platforms is so important.

Remember the example from earlier in the book about not buying television advertising during a morning game show program and airing a commercial aimed at college students? That decision is based on the relevance of the marketing campaign to the target audience. The same is true of social media. As a first step, choosing your social media platforms carefully will help to ensure the relevance of your content.

Text content without visuals, for example, will do much better on Facebook or Twitter than on Instagram or Pinterest. Likewise, content aimed at teens will do better on

Snapchat than on Facebook, since teens use Facebook less than other demographic groups.

Once you've figured out which social media platforms are best, relevance depends on the subject of your content. Is it interesting to your target audience? Does it address problems or questions that they have in their daily lives? Which ones? Does it promote products or services that they use or would want to use? Does it show them why they should want to use a new product or service that they have not used before? Why or why not? Does it showcase your brand in a way that is appealing to them? In what way?

These questions are specific to your target demographic, and no two companies will have the same answers. It's valuable to explore the answers to these questions in order to ensure that you are creating social media marketing that is relevant to your target audience.

Luckily, there is a secret to making sure that your content is relevant to your target demographic: consume what they're consuming. If you can figure out what type of already existing content your target demographic likes best, you can better tailor your content to what they prefer.

Here, you can get much more specific rather than simply relying on the age bracket demographics described in the previous chapter. Rather than "young professionals," you can research "young professionals in finance in the New York area." Instead of "older but not yet retired consumers" you can look at "older but not yet retired farmers in the western US." The possibilities are endless. For a large company marketing a broad product that could appeal to large groups of people, this sort of research might result in a multi-pronged marketing campaign that targets different segments of people in different ways.

For a small company with a more specific product, this research allows them to better target the group they know to be their primary consumers. In short, figure out what is attractive to your target audience, and then become attractive to them.

Quality

As more and more people produce content to put online and video and camera technology becomes cheaper, the overall quality of what is found on social media is going up. From a social media marketing perspective, this means your brand has to keep up. You don't have to have a full production studio with actors and a green screen to create quality content for social media, but chances are that your old point-and-shoot digital camera isn't going to cut it, and the video editing software that came free on your laptop might not be quite what you're needing. It used to be that anyone could make a low-quality home video.

These days, just about anyone can make a medium-quality home video good enough to post on YouTube. Amateurs with their own vlogs and a little video editing software can make content that rivals some companies. You don't have to try to beat Hollywood, but it's important not to skimp on the basics when producing content for social media marketing. Consumers are very good judges of the effort that went into making an image or video, and most of the time, poorly-produced content will get buried rather than getting shared.

For images, make sure you know your social media platform. Facebook supports both vertical (portrait) and horizontal (landscape) images. Pinterest works better with portrait-oriented images, while Instagram is famous for its square image format. Images on

Snapchat can be in either portrait or landscape orientation, but the platform is designed primarily for portrait-style photos.

Most of the filters and lenses on Snapchat require photographs to be taken vertically in order to fit or to have the added text face the correct direction. More importantly, Snapchat users expect photos to be vertically oriented. If they come across a horizontally oriented photo, they will have to turn their smartphone to face the right way. This might seem like a small adjustment to make, but remember that social media users often expect instant gratification. They might simply tap through that horizontal photo without looking at it. To make sure your content gets viewed on Snapchat, keep it vertical.

For video, the same considerations apply. Videos on Facebook can be vertical or horizontal, while those on Instagram are square. YouTube is designed to support horizontal video, and vertical videos uploaded to the site don't look as good. In contrast, vertical video is preferred on Snapchat where, like with images, the platform's features are designed to be more compatible with a vertical orientation.

For content on some social media platforms, such as Facebook, YouTube, Instagram, and Pinterest, your company may want to hire a professional photographer, videographer, or graphic designer. Having good equipment does make a difference in the quality of the final product, and a professional can help you make images or videos that really stand out.

However, for Snapchat and to some extent Instagram, having a real employee rather than an artist or professional behind the content you share is actually a benefit. Snapchat is popular with young people because it shows unfiltered, real life events as they happen. One common criticism of many social media platforms is that they show a carefully curated image of a user's life or, in this case, a company's product. Snapchat allows users to step outside that image and share their lives as they happen.

Because Snapchat users value this realistic image, they are more likely to connect with your company if someone who works there, rather than a hired videographer, is in charge of your Snapchat story. The same can be true of Instagram, though to a lesser extent.

Instagram is frequently a top target of people who claim that social media presents a fake image of a user's life, but it can also showcase little everyday moments at your company in a way that other platforms cannot.
In addition, the app's built in photo and video editing capabilities means you can do some of that work yourself.

In general, when it comes to quality, make sure that the content you produce for your social media marketing campaign is attractive and showcases your company's best attributes, but also stay conscious of the social media platform you are using. The way to show your company's best attributes with a YouTube video is not the same way you would use in a Facebook post or a Snapchat story. It's a lot to keep track of at first, but as you get to know the different social media platforms, you will be able to more easily figure out what content to share and how to produce it.

Storytelling

Storytelling is a technique to keep the content you produce for social media marketing interesting. Imagine, for a moment, that you're trying to promote a daily planner. Maybe it's a particularly nice daily planner, but there are a lot of other daily planners available and most of them are fairly similar to yours. To advertise your planner, you could try to point out all of the ways in which it is different and better than the other planners.

A video about it might start with some nice images of your planner, followed by a voiceover or video of an actor talking about how great it is. Maybe it has brighter colors, more writing space, and a built-in page marker. Maybe it's pocket-size. Maybe it's made with recycled paper.

Does this sound boring to you yet? The problem with marketing that simply lists the attributes of the product being promoted is that it just isn't that interesting to consumers. Consider your own social media account, if you have one.

If you came across a video about a daily planner like the one described above, would you stop scrolling through your feed long enough to watch it? It's possible that people who are particularly interested in daily planners might, but chances are that such a generic video would not attract a lot of attention.

Now imagine, instead, that your video about the daily planner depicts a busy family with working parents and involved kids. You watch the family going about their day and you realize that the parents have completely forgotten about their daughter's soccer match that evening.

They've promised to be there, and you see the daughter waiting impatiently on the sidelines as the minutes tick down to the start of the game. And then, just when you think that everything is going to end in catastrophe, the parents glance at their daily planner and remember that they need to be at the game. They arrive just in time, and the planner saves the day!

It's a very simple, and in many ways predictable, story line. Yet that video would be far more interesting than the first video, and it would also be more memorable. In addition, viewers are far more likely to be hooked by the second video, about a family, when scrolling through their social media feed. Many people have families, and they are more likely to identify with marketing that references their reality. In short, even

the most simplistic storytelling narrative can make for more attractive marketing than an advertisement that does not use storytelling.

How you use storytelling for social media marketing will depend on your brand, the social media platform, and your target demographic. Different social media platforms support certain types of media better than others, so you might tell a story in a series of images on

Pinterest, with a video on Youtube (cross-posted to Facebook and Twitter), and with a series of videos on your Snap Story. To come up with a story, get creative. Have a brainstorming session about narratives that might work well with your brand. Include your co-workers. You can even involve your social media network in this process. Facebook allows users to create polls, or you could simply make a post asking them what your brand reminds them of. You might be surprised by the answers you receive, and some may be great starting points for a marketing campaign.

Using storytelling for social media marketing has the added benefit of creating enduring characters that can be used for multiple marketing campaigns. To go back to the example of the daily planner, imagine that the video of the family with the soccer-playing daughter was well received and resulted in successful sales increases for your company.

For your next video, you could continue to feature the same family or members of the family in different contexts. Videos could depict the mom or dad at work or the daughter at school with her friends. Using the same characters will help consumers link your new videos back to your initial video, reinforcing the image of your brand that you are trying to create.

Storytelling connects well with the consumers you are trying to reach because it is more in line with how people interact with each other on a daily basis. If you call a friend to

tell him or her about something that happened at work, you will usually start with an introduction, introduce a problem or even that occurred, and end with the resolution of the problem or the end of the workday. Marketing that follows this same narrative connects more easily with viewers because it's a formula they are used to.

Storytelling also connects ideas with emotions. Think back to the original example advertisements about the daily planner. The first ad, just listing the attributes of the

planner, didn't arouse any emotions in the viewer. The second ad, in contrast, made the viewer feel apprehension about the situation presented in the video.

Would the parents realize that their daughter had a soccer match in time to make it to the big game? That apprehension is then followed by an emotional release when the problem is resolved, resulting in a happy ending. By appealing to emotions, storytelling helps to shut off the part of the brain that deals with rational considerations. If presented with a list of the qualities of a great daily planner, you might respond with rational arguments for why you don't need a daily planner, or why the daily planner presented in the video isn't the right one for you. However, if you've been caught up in an emotional narrative, you're no longer thinking about these rational considerations, and you're more likely to think about purchasing the daily planner depicted.

The story you tell with your social media marketing doesn't have to relate directly to the product you're selling. Even telling a compelling story in conjunction with the promotion of your product can be enough. This is the idea behind getting star athletes to advertise various products. Olympic runners may or may not eat Wheaties for breakfast, but associating the breakfast cereal with a great sports story helps people to connect with the brand.

The most important part of storytelling as a part of social media marketing is to recount a narrative that people can relate to. Be authentic. Keep your story simple. Make sure it has universal appeal. Get in touch with emotions. Those are the keys to successful storytelling and successful social media marketing.

Chapter 6: Networking Makes Your Content Go Farther

It's the number one rule of job hunting today: network, network, network. And it's the number one rule of social media marketing today, too. Social media is just that: social. Unlike those television commercials of the past, where companies talked *at* their consumers and consumers listened, social media marketing needs to talk *with* those consumers.

Creating a back-and-forth between your brand and other social media users is key to success with social media marketing. Remember the importance of the shareability factor? If another social media user know you and your brand, they are more likely to share your content. And what better way to get them to know you and your brand than sharing their content in the first place?

Social media is all about karma. Posts that get liked and shared more get promoted more highly in the algorithms that determine what social media users see first in their feeds and on their home pages. Liking and sharing another user's content or following them on social media not only introduces them to your brand, but also gives them a boost. Chances are they will be appreciative of your attention and like, share, or follow you back. And this rule goes both ways. If someone likes, shares, or follows you, do the same to them. What goes around comes around, and by being an active participant in the social media community, you will gain much more attention than by simply existing on a social media platform.

If you're not sure how to start making use of social media karma, begin by seeking out other users of social media platforms that do what you do, or who might be interested in what you do. For example, if you are a small, local shop that sells high-quality kitchen equipment, find the other shops in your neighborhood on Facebook and give them a like.

Follow some restaurants in your city on Twitter and Instagram, and re-pin their content on Pinterest. Make existing content about your business go farther by sharing it on social media platforms other than the one it was originally posted on. If a local newspaper published an article about you, share it on Facebook, Twitter, and even LinkedIn.

If someone posted a picture from your business on Instagram, like it and share it on Facebook (you might not always be able to do this, however, depending on individual privacy settings). If you're really just getting started, you might consider getting in touch with some people you know and asking them to like or follow you on a social media platform. Especially if these are people who are already familiar with your company, they are likely to be happy to help out. After all, what goes around comes around. If they ever need help with social media promotion in the future, they will know they can count on you for a boost.

Chapter 7: Going the Distance with Social Media Marketing

Social media is one of those things that is tempting to neglect. Once you've created a stellar Facebook page, Twitter profile, or Pinterest Board for your company, you might be tempted to sit back and let the internet do its work. However, social media marketing does not do well with a "get it and forget it" attitude. Just like traditional marketing, social media marketing takes work. In some cases, it takes even more work.

Instead of allowing you to create a marketing campaign, unleash it on the public, then sit back to watch it do its job, social media marketing requires frequent or even daily participation in the community you have joined. Some platforms are more forgiving than others on this point, but the key point is the same: if you do not stay present and accessible on social media, any followers you have gained will eventually drop away.

Social media users are fickle because they can be. There is so much content created on a daily basis that if something is not satisfying to them, they will find another source. Don't let your followers consider going somewhere else. Keep them interested with regular updates. Respond in a timely manner to likes, follows, retweets, and other interactions. Don't let yourself get complacent, because the rewards from persistent social media marketing are worth it.

Being active on social media means different things for different social media platforms. For each of the social media platforms discussed in previous chapters, here is an idea of how often it is a good idea to be active. Each platform is rated in terms of speed. A fast social media platform requires very regular, often more than daily, activity. A slow social media platform only requires updates every few days. Most social media platforms fall somewhere in between.

Facebook

Facebook is a medium-fast social media platform. While it's not necessary for your company to post updates or content every single day, the sheer volume of material on Facebook means that posts get buried very quickly. The more often you are able to update, the more likely your posts are to be seen before they are covered by newer content. Luckily, Facebook supports content from other social media networks, so you can share photos or videos from Instagram, videos from YouTube, and images from Pinterest on Facebook. It's good to get in the habit of cross-posting to Facebook every time you use one of these other social media platforms. This interconnectedness helps people find your company on all of the social media platforms that you use, increasing your number of followers.

Twitter

Twitter is a medium-fast social media platform for many of the same reasons as Facebook. The quantity of content produced on the site means that you have to post regularly to be seen. This problem is exacerbated by the limited length of tweets. It's good to be active on Twitter every day, even if only by reacting to or retweeting other users' posts. Again, it's possible to cross-post to Twitter, so make multiple uses of content you have produced for other social media platforms.

YouTube

YouTube is a medium-slow social media platform. While YouTube videos make great content to share on other social media platforms such as Facebook and Twitter, you don't have to produce them every day. Especially if you are going a more traditional route and hiring a videographer to depict your company, you may not want to be posting videos that regularly. However, if video is a good media for showing what your company does, and you have the ability to create content for YouTube frequently, don't hesitate to make use of that.

YouTube, more than most other social media platforms, has been a starting point for fame for plenty of ordinary people with a video camera and good ideas. Just don't forget to cross-post!

LinkedIn

LinkedIn is a slow social media platform. Because it focuses more on professional content, it is not as flooded as Facebook and Twitter with images and articles. Being active on

LinkedIn is a great way to make connections with other companies and professionals, but you don't have to post every day. Sharing an interesting, relevant article or posting a message promoting your company once or twice a week is likely enough to keep active on the platform. However, if your field uses LinkedIn more regularly, don't hesitate to be more active. Keep up with what your peers on LinkedIn are posting and you will be on the right track.

Instagram

Instagram is a medium social media platform. Many people carefully curate their Instagram profiles, meaning that they do not post as regularly as they might to Facebook or Twitter. Taking the perfect image and editing it requires time. This gives you some flexibility in how you want to use Instagram for social media marketing. Posting every day will give you an edge, but you can also take some extra time to make sure your photos and videos are top notch. Try to post three to four times a week to make sure not to fall off the radars of your followers.

Snapchat

Snapchat is a fast social media platform, especially if you are publishing a public Snap Story. The best Snap Stories are updated several times a day, or even several times an hour. If you commit to creating a public Snap Story, you may want to have a designated person in charge of the Story.

Unlike on other social media platforms, where you have a profile, on Snapchat, if you don't post content, you almost don't exist. On the other hand, Snapchat offers a flexibility and a sense of proximity that other social media platforms just don't allow. If you decide

that Snapchat is the right social media platform for your social media marketing campaign, make sure to keep up!

Pinterest

Pinterest is a medium-slow social media platform. Because users search for Pins, it's less imperative that you post content regularly. On the other hand, Pinterest users do have home pages featuring recent Pins and Boards from the users they follow. Getting your content on these home pages is good. Luckily, Pinterest is the ultimate cross-posting site.

In fact, the site is designed to aggregate content from other websites and social media platforms. Make use of this feature and cross-post any image from any other social media platform to Pinterest. You can also use Pinterest to post images from your company website. Even better, it's a quick and easy process to do so, meaning that Pinterest, more than most other social media platforms, does allow you to sit back and relax a bit.

There will almost certainly come a moment in your social media marketing journey when you get very tired of coming up with content, cross-posting to multiple platforms, and keeping up with what your followers like. This is especially true if you are a smaller business with less experience marketing. Don't get discouraged, and don't quit. Social media marketing isn't easy. There's a lot of competition out there. Never forget that you have the tools at hand in this book to create a great social media marketing campaign. If you need to take a couple days off and regroup, give yourself permission to do so. But then, log back and and keep posting, liking, and sharing. It makes a big difference in the long run.

Conclusion

Thank you for finishing this book on social media marketing! With the help of the information in these chapters, you are hopefully well on your way to having a successful social media marketing campaign, no matter your brand or the product you are promoting.

While this book is a great start, it is not an exhaustive review of social media marketing for every social media platform that exists. Depending on your product or target audience, you may want to explore some of the many other social media platforms that exist. Reddit, Tumblr, Flickr, and even Google+ can be useful in some cases.

There may even be industry-specific social media platforms or groups that would be relevant to your business. Once you get going with social media marketing, don't stop here. Keep exploring, making connections, and expanding your reach on social media. A short time ago, the marketing possibilities that exist on social media would have been unimaginable. Only time will tell what possibilities will exist in the future.

If you found this book useful in any way, don't hesitate to leave a review on Amazon! We appreciate it.